Guide to
Textbook Publishing Contracts

Stephen E. Gillen

Guide to Textbook Publishing Contracts
By Stephen E. Gillen
Copyright © 2016 by Textbook & Academic Authors Association (TAA)

For further information contact:

Textbook & Academic Authors Association (TAA)
PO Box 367, Fountain City, WI 54629. Phone: (727) 563-0020 Email: Info@TAAonline.net Website: TAAonline.net

The information and advice in this book are accurate and effective to the best of our knowledge but are offered without guarantee. The author and Textbook & Academic Authors Association disclaim all liability in connection with the use of this book.

Publisher: Textbook & Academic Authors Association (TAA)
Project Manager: Kim Pawlak, Director of Publishing & Operations, TAA
Cover and Interior Design/Composition: Laurie A. Nelson, Marketing Manager, TAA

© iStockphoto © Adobe Stock

ISBN 978-0-9975004-0-0

The Textbook & Academic Authors Association (TAA) provides a wide range of professional development resources, events, and networking opportunities for textbook authors and authors of scholarly journal articles and books. TAA's mission is to support textbook and academic authors in the creation of top-quality educational and scholarly works that stimulate the love of learning and foster the pursuit of knowledge. Its members are aspiring, new, and veteran textbook authors and authors of scholarly journal articles and books and come from a wide range of disciplines. Visit us at TAAonline.net.

Table of Contents

"20 Questions to Ask Your Editor"

BONUS MATERIAL

Introduction

If you've ever been published, then you've seen it before — a *WHEREAS* and a *THEREFORE* followed by eight or more pages of pre-printed, pedantic prose offered up by the editor as his/her "standard publishing contract." Other than a few tiny spaces for your name, the title of the work, and the manuscript delivery date, the bulk of it looks as though it were long ago locked down in Century Schoolbook type.

But the truth is that there is more to review than the spelling of your name, choice of title, and projected completion date, and more to negotiate than you might realize or believe. Authors, you see, (particularly first-time authors) are an insecure lot. As often as not, you have toiled in isolation, hour after hour, wondering all the while whether your proposal or manuscript is good enough to get past the slush pile. More often than not, your anxiety is then validated by rejection after rejection until finally, for the good who are also lucky, a receptive editor signals an interest.

You Have More Leverage Than You Think

Editors are under ever increasing pressure to sign new titles, meet publication dates, and deliver sales results. For many of them, these factors have a direct bearing on their year-end compensation (a circumstance that can work to your significant bargaining advantage as year-end approaches). While there are many aspiring first-time authors out there, only a relative handful will be published. If you have attracted interest or a contract offer, then you have already made the first cut. A reasonable list of tactfully stated concerns and requested amendments will only reinforce the impression that you are a competent and thorough professional. Moreover, the editor will have invested a significant amount of time in reviewing your proposal, perhaps getting outside reviews, preparing a pro forma profit and loss analysis, and drafting a publication plan and recommendation for his/her superiors — if you are not signed, all of this effort will have been for naught and the editor will be back to square one.

You Have to Do Your Homework

Negotiations are ultimately influenced by which side knows the most about the other side's positions. The editor starts this contest with an advantage gained from experience in the market, experience doing other similar deals (undoubtedly many more than you have done), and the benefits of your perspective as reflected in your proposal. The way to get on an even footing with the editor/publisher is to learn more about the publisher's plans for, and expectations of, your work — information that will help you evaluate your leverage and the editor's weaknesses. Ask about these issues in the context of negotiating a book contract and the editor will evade them, hedge, or refuse to answer. Ask about them after the editor has indicated an interest in your work but before you engage in active, contract-focused negotiations — in the context of learning more about the editor/publisher, more about their list and their business, more about the market and your potential competition — and you may catch the editor still in his or her selling mode. Ask them yourself, in person or over the phone, (rather than through your lawyer) and you are more likely to get candid responses. Negotiations may be formal and may be best handled by your lawyer in order to preserve your relationship with your editor. But information gathering will be most effective if you do it in person. It may take some prodding, probing, wheedling, and cajoling, but the information you gather will prove valuable, so make sure you take copious notes.

> **The way to get on an even footing** with the editor/publisher is to learn more about the publisher's plans for, and expectations of, your work...

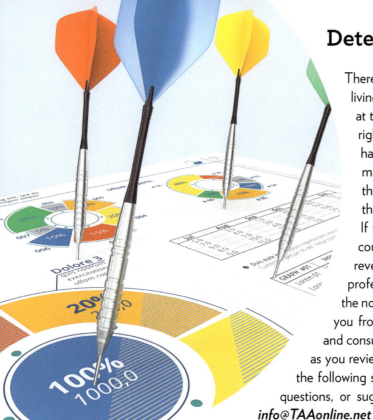

Determine What's Important to You

There is no one-size-fits-all solution. If you make your primary living as a professional writer, then money issues will likely be at the top of your list — advances, grants, royalties, and re-use rights should be the focus of your attention. If, on the other hand, you are an academic living by the "publish or perish" mantra and in search of the inner peace that tenure will bring, then the money issues may well take a back seat to ensuring that your work is actually published — on schedule and intact. If you are a professional of another sort (doctor, lawyer, accountant, consultant) and you view the book not so much as a revenue generator, but more as a promotional piece and as your professional *bona fides*, then your principal focus may well be on the non-compete provision and ensuring that it does not preclude you from engaging in the kind of professional writing, speaking, and consulting that does pay the bills. Keep your goals firmly in mind as you review the clauses and the better/best alternatives discussed in the following sections of this book. And if you have additional thoughts, questions, or suggestions for improving this guide, please send them to *info@TAAonline.net*

There is no one-size-fits-all solution. Keep your goals firmly in mind as you review the clauses and the better/best alternatives discussed in this book.

Key Provisions
of a Typical Textbook Contract

Please note: This document is an informational guide to textbook contracts. It includes specimen language from a variety of more or less typical textbook contracts from a variety of sources, but it is not a "model" contract. It can be used by the author to engage in a more informed manner in the negotiating process. As you will see from the clause-by-clause discussion that follows, not every provision in the publisher's typical contract is equally deserving of attention and some don't need attention at all.

1. Preamble

The preamble is the paragraph at the top of the contract where the parties are identified, the date of the agreement is noted, and sometimes the purpose is described. Some authors may wish to enter the contract in the name of a personal services limited liability company or close corporation for tax or estate planning purposes. If this is the case, you will want to get professional advice first, because a mistake in the contract or process may frustrate your objectives. See (1.) for a typical preamble in a textbook contract.

This Agreement, effective this _____ day of _____, 20___, between [insert name of publisher], having its principal place of business at [insert address of publisher], (the "Publisher") and [insert name of author #1] whose address is [insert address of author #1], a citizen of _____ (country), whose year of birth is _____ and whose Federal Tax I.D. No. is _____ and [insert name of author #2] whose address is [insert address of author #2], a citizen of _____(country), whose year of birth is _____ and whose Federal Tax I.D. No. is _____ (individually or collectively the "Author," except that the warranties and indemnities created in Section XX shall apply individually to each author's contributions to the Work).

2. Grant of Rights by the Author to the Publisher

The grant of rights clause spells out the breadth of rights being acquired by the publisher — and there is a broad range of possibilities here. The provision in (2a.) is typical of what is generally provided in a textbook publisher's form agreement.

Least favorable to the author are "work-for-hire" provisions (like the one in 2a.), which transfer the broadest possible rights to the publisher and deprive the author of certain statutory protections. While relatively uncommon

Grant of Rights. The Author acknowledges that the Work was specially commissioned by the Publisher and intended as an instructional text and agrees that the Work shall be considered a work-made-for-hire, with the Publisher deemed the author and sole owner thereof for copyright purposes. In addition, and against the possibility that the Work might ultimately be deemed incapable of characterization as a work-made-for-hire as a matter of law, the author hereby irrevocably grants to the Publisher all right, title and interest (including, without limitation, all copyrights throughout the world and all other legal and equitable rights in all media, whether now known or hereafter invented) to the Work. The Author acknowledges that she/he shall not acquire any rights of any kind in the Work as a result of his/her services under this Agreement.

in trade book deals, they are often used in educational publishing (especially at lower curricular levels). More common (and slightly more favorable to the author) are grants of "all right, title, and interest," (also included in (2a.), as the publisher's fallback position in the event the work at issue does not qualify for work-for-hire treatment). While appearing to be all encompassing, the "all rights" grant at least leaves the author with her/his statutory protections intact. But in the final analysis, there is little reason for the publisher to get rights that it does not intend to exploit. If your publisher intends only to publish an eBook edition for distribution in North America, then the grant of rights should arguably convey North American eBook rights only. Alternate editions can be addressed by amendment to your book contract if and when the publisher expresses an interest in publishing them. As a practical matter, however, most publishers are unlikely to give much ground here because of uncertainty about how the market is evolving and what the distribution media and channels of the future will be.

The following provisions (2b. and 2c.) represent possible compromises that allocate rights in the work more equitably. Getting a publisher to compromise on this issue may be a tough sell, but that's no reason not to ask – the only certainty here is that you will not get that for which you do not ask.

2b. Conditional Grant of Rights - better

Conditional Grant of All Rights. The Author hereby grants to the Publisher the sole and exclusive right and license to publish, promote, distribute and sell (or permit others to do so) the Work in all languages, in all media, and throughout the world; provided, however, that the right to publish the Work in any form other than eBook form (the "Subsidiary Rights") shall become non-exclusive as to those Subsidiary Rights which have not been commercially exploited by the Publisher within two years after first publication of the Work in book form and the Author expressly reserves the non-exclusive right also to exploit said unexercised Subsidiary Rights, free of any obligation to pay royalties to the Publisher, but agrees to cooperate with the Publisher to ensure that any such exploitation shall not interfere with the Publisher's exclusive right to produce and publish the Work in book form.

2c. Grant of Exclusive Book Publishing Rights - better still

Grant of Exclusive Book Publishing Rights. The Author hereby grants to the Publisher the sole and exclusive right and license to publish, promote, distribute and sell (or permit others to do so) the Work in the English language only, in printed book form only, and only for distribution in North America. All other rights in the Work are expressly reserved exclusively to the Author.

Negotiating Strategy:

In this day and age, most publishers are in fact positioned to exploit (through subsidiaries, affiliates, and standing relationships) more than book publishing rights and it is in your best interest to let them have everything they will effectively commercialize. The extent to which you bargain to retain some of these rights will depend upon the nature of your work and whether it lends itself to these alternative uses, the publisher's ability and interest in exploiting them for you, and your ability to do this independently.

But you should resist the temptation to get sloppy here and you should endeavor to force the publisher to specify which, if any, of the following rights it truly needs and is presently positioned to exploit, including:

- Hardcover

- Soft cover

- eBook

- Custom publishing

- Bundling

- Rentals

- Incorporation in a digital database or integrated learning system

- Audio (books on tape)

- Translation

- English language adaptation

The list of possibilities goes on and on. To the extent these rights are licensed by the publisher to some other, they are referred to as "subsidiary rights" (i.e., rights subsidiary to the publisher's principal line of business).

3. A Word About Royalties

Understanding royalties and royalty accounting can be a daunting task for the uninitiated, as the fairly typical provision demonstrates in (3a).

3a. Royalties - typical

Royalties. Except as otherwise provided below, the Publisher will pay to the Author a royalty of _____% based upon the Publisher's net receipts from sales by it of copies of the Work, revisions thereof, or reprints of all or portions thereof. A royalty at one half the aforementioned rate will be applied to the Publisher's net receipts:

(a) from sales by it in foreign markets of special editions, adaptations, or regular editions of the Work, or from sales by it in the domestic or foreign markets of foreign language editions or adaptations of the Work;

(b) from sales by it of visual or sound reproductions or adaptations, motion pictures, educational and commercial television versions, braille and largetype editions, microfilm or microfiche editions, and microcomputer adaptations of the Work;

(c) from the sales by its subsidiaries or business affiliates through trade channels, mail order or coupon advertising campaigns, and solicitation by radio and television.

(d) from the Publisher's use or adaptation of the Work (or any portion thereof) in conjunction with any other work as a part of a database or custom published work through any means of storage, transmission, or copying now known or hereafter devised. With respect to this subsection (d), the Author's royalty shall be applied to a pro rata portion of the net receipts, said portion to be determined through use of a reasonable and objective method of relative valuation to be selected by the Publisher in its sole discretion.

The Publisher will pay to the Author 50% of the Publisher's net proceeds:

(e) from agreements to transfer, sell, or license to others the right to reprint all or portions of the Work, to include the Work in an electronic database, or to make visual or sound reproductions or adaptations, motion pictures, educational and commercial television versions, Braille and large-type editions, microfilm, or microfiche editions, microcomputer adaptations, electronic versions, translations, or foreign editions or adaptations either in English or in foreign languages.

No royalty shall be paid on copies sold at a discount of more than 50% or below the cost of manufacture. Publisher may set up a reserve sufficient in its opinion to allow for returns.

The royalty clause generally provides for a base rate on the cash actually received by the publisher from sales though its traditional distribution channels, with much lower rates on sales through a number of secondary channels. Over the last decade, it has become common for publishers to provide for some discretionary mechanism for allocating the sales proceeds from special bundling deals and from exploitation of electronic rights (d). On rights sales (e) as opposed to product sales, the publisher typically splits the proceeds 50/50 with the author. Sometimes the publisher takes a larger share; only with some significant effort will you get the publisher to take less. Understanding these provisions means understanding the publisher's distribution and accounting models, which can be labyrinthine. Include an audit clause, and leave unraveling the maze to the sharp pencils.

3b. Royalties - better

Royalties. Except as otherwise provided below, the Publisher will pay to the Author a royalty of:

_____% on the first _____ copies in any single edition

_____% on the next _____ copies in any single edition

_____% on all copies thereafter in any single edition

based upon the Publisher's net receipts from sales by it of copies of the Work, revisions thereof, or reprints of all or portions thereof ("net receipts" means cash received by the Publisher less returns, exchanges, and any amounts separately itemized on the customer's invoice for shipping, handling, or taxes). Author shall have the right, upon reasonable notice and during usual business hours but not more than once each year, to have the books and records of Publisher examined at the place where the same are regularly maintained insofar as they relate to the Work, by an independent public accountant. Such examination shall be at the cost of Author unless the net of all errors aggregate to more than three percent (3%) of the total sum accrued to Author are found to Author's disadvantage, in which case the cost of such examination shall be borne by Publisher. Any amounts disclosed by the examination to be due to the Author shall be promptly paid together with interest at the rate of ___% per month calculated from the date the payment should have been made.

Negotiating Strategy:

Royalties are the proverbial two birds in the bush. Far better to negotiate for non-refundable advances — these represent a bird in the hand and, if they are significant, increase the publisher's stake in promoting your work to ensure its commercial success. In textbook deals, your rate will most likely be calculated on net receipts (cover price is more common in trade book deals). Be sure, however, that the "net" in net receipts is clearly defined so you know what will be deducted. Also ask for a copy of the publisher's discount schedule and for some historical averages (i.e., how much of the publisher's sales are typically done at each discount rate) so that you can compare apples to apples in the event you are the happy holder of two or more contract offers. What is a good royalty rate and how much should you ask for? Unfortunately, there is no pat answer to this question, though a decades old 1200-respondent survey conducted by the National Writers Union concluded that textbook rates range from as low as 5% for K-6 to as high as 20% for some college and graduate level works and a more recent, but smaller *(403-respondent), survey* conducted by TAA and Digital Book Pioneer and Industry Expert June Parsons, indicated a range from below 9% to 30% with the most common range from 10% to 18%. If you do your homework, you will at least be able to ask for a tiered royalty structure — a base rate up to the publisher's break even volume, a higher rate on sales over break even, and a higher rate still on sales over the volume at which the publisher achieves its target margin.

Royalties are the proverbial two birds in the bush. Far better to negotiate for non-refundable advances — these represent a bird in the hand and, if they are significant, increase the publisher's stake in promoting your work to ensure its commercial success.

Royalties. Except as otherwise provided below, the Publisher will pay to the Author a royalty of:

_____% on the first _____ copies in any single edition

_____% on the next _____ copies in any single edition

_____% on all copies thereafter in any single edition

based upon the cover price of the Work and revisions and reprints thereof.

The Publisher will pay to the Author 50% of the Publisher's net proceeds from agreements to transfer, sell, or license to others the right to exercise any of the Subsidiary Rights granted herein. Author shall have the right, upon reasonable notice and during usual business hours but not more than once each year, to have the books and records of Publisher examined at the place where the same are regularly maintained insofar as they relate to the Work, by an independent public accountant. Such examination shall be at the cost of Author unless the net of all errors aggregate to more than three percent (3%) of the total sum accrued to Author are found to Author's disadvantage, in which case the cost of such examination shall be borne by Publisher. Any amounts disclosed by the examination to be due to the Author shall be promptly paid together with interest at the rate of ___% per month calculated from the date the payment should have been made.

4. Advances and Grants

An advance is a pre-payment of royalties to be earned upon the publication of your textbook. It will be recouped out of the royalties first accrued from the commercial exploitation of your work. It is not uncommon for publishers to agree to advance from 50% to 100% of expected royalties on projected first year sales. The advance may or may not be re-fundable if your manuscript is rejected and your contract is cancelled.

A grant, conversely, is a payment intended to cover some or all of the out-of-pocket costs of research and/or manuscript preparation. It is generally not recouped out of accrued royalties and, like the advance, may or may not be refundable in the event the manuscript is rejected.

If you are successful in obtaining substantial advances, be sure that they are paid upon submission of manuscript (and not on the publisher's acceptance, which might be delayed) and that they are not cross-collateralized (i.e., recoverable from royalties earned by other titles that you might have written or might yet write for the same publisher – see italicized language in example 4a.). Since grants are intended to offset or reimburse expenses, some portion should be disbursed right away to get you started and the remainder should be disbursed as you provide evidence of expenses incurred. Grants should not be refundable, even if your manuscript is rejected.

4a. Advances and Grants - typical

ADVANCES: On this first edition of the Work only, the Publisher shall pay to the Author as an advance the sum of $XX,XXX, as follows:

$X,XXX upon the signing of this Agreement by all parties;

$X,XXX upon Publisher's acceptance of a complete first draft of the manuscript; and

$X,XXX upon Publisher's acceptance of a complete and acceptable final draft of the manuscript;

provided, however, that the Publisher shall be entitled to recover said advance out of the royalties and other sums first otherwise due to the Author pursuant to this *or any other* contract between them.

GRANTS: On this first edition of the Work only, the Publisher shall pay to the Author, as a non-recoupable grant to defray the cost of research and manuscript preparation, the sum of $X,XXX, as follows:

$X,XXX upon the signing of this Agreement by all parties;

$X,XXX upon Publisher's acceptance of a complete first draft of the manuscript; and

$X,XXX upon Publisher's acceptance of a complete and acceptable final draft of the manuscript.

Grants should not be refundable, even if your manuscript is rejected.

ADVANCES: On this first edition of the Work only, the Publisher shall pay to the Author as an advance the sum of $XX,XXX, as follows:

$X,XXX upon the signing of this Agreement by all parties;

$X,XXX upon delivery of a complete first draft of the manuscript; and

$X,XXX upon delivery of a complete and acceptable final draft of the manuscript;

provided, however, that the Publisher shall be entitled to recover said advance out of the royalties and other sums first otherwise due to the Author pursuant to this Agreement.

GRANTS: On this first edition of the Work only, the Publisher shall pay to the Author, as a non-recoupable grant to defray the cost of research and manuscript preparation, the sum of up to $X,XXX, as follows:

$X,XXX upon the signing of this Agreement by all parties;

with the remainder upon the Author's submission of evidence of qualifying disbursements.

5. Electronic Rights

If the grant language in your contract acknowledges creation of the work as a work-for-hire or if it consists of an assignment of the entire contract (the first and second examples 4a. and 4b.), then electronic rights are included in the transfer without more being said. Some 1970s vintage and earlier contracts conveyed "book publishing rights." Because some of these older books are still selling as classics, courts have been asked on a couple of occasions to determine whether the "book" in "book publishing rights" is only a print book or whether it encompasses also the eBook form. The resulting decisions have been highly fact dependent and have split as a result. Suffice to say, that it is important to be clear about the rights being granted and that most post-1970s publishing contracts have consequently provided expressly for eBook rights and have gone further to encompass rights in all media and by all means, whether now known or hereafter developed.

Although electronic rights are often discussed as though they were one homogenous format, the truth is that they range from an eBook that is little more than a PDF version of the printed text to a fully integrated learning system. The business and pricing models are different from that for printed books for many reasons, among them that re-sales are much less of an issue and manufacturing and distribution costs can be much less. But although the market is clearly headed in the

direction of digital formats, progress is slow and those sales are still a small fraction of total sales. Because unit volumes are low, up-front costs must be spread over a smaller base and are for that reason more of a factor. The norm for royalty rates in this market is that the rate for revenue from digital sales is the same as the rate for domestic sales of the print edition. You may hear that publishers are paying 25% of net receipts on eBook sales, but it is only the trade book publishers who are doing this and rates in that market tend to be about double what textbook publishers are paying. You may also hear that because eBooks are technically licensed and not sold, this revenue stream is more like the subsidiary rights revenue from third party licenses, which is generally split 50/50 between publisher and author. Although this may be technically accurate where eBook sales are effected through an intermediary, as a larger percentage of the publisher's business moves to this channel, paying an overarching 50% royalty is probably not a sustainable business model for them.

Electronic rights often range from an eBook that is little more than a PDF version of the printed text to a fully integrated learning system.

6. Copyright

Most textbook contracts will provide that the publisher may register the copyright in the name of the publisher. Although there might under certain limited circumstances be an advantage to the author to holding the copyrights in his/her name, as a practical matter this is probably not an issue worth doing battle over. The publisher is in the best position to handle the registration and to police and enforce the claim. In the event the book is allowed to go out of print, the publisher will revert ownership of the copyrights and the registrations to the author.

7. Competing Publications

Almost every publishing contract will include a "non-compete" provision as shown in (7a), calculated to ensure that the publisher has a monopoly on your work on a particular subject and that you do not publish or assist in publishing any other work that might compete.

These restrictions are usually very broadly drafted and open-ended in scope. As such, they may be unenforceable as an unreasonable restraint of trade. Better, however, to try to narrow them before you sign.

7a. Competing Publications - typical

COMPETING WORKS. During the life of this Agreement, the Author will not without the prior written consent of the Publisher participate in the preparation or publication of any work on a similar subject, which might tend in the sole and absolute judgment of the publisher to interfere with or injure the sale of the Work, and will not authorize the use of the Author's name in connection with any such work.

7b. Competing Publications - better

COMPETING WORKS. During the life of this Agreement, the Author will not without the prior written consent of the Publisher participate in the preparation or publication of any directly competing work. For purposes of this Section, a "directly competing work" shall be defined as any book-length work on the subject of [be as specific as possible].

7c. Competing Publications - better still

COMPETING WORKS. During the life of this Agreement, the Author will not without the prior written consent of the Publisher participate in the preparation or publication of any directly competing work. For purposes of this Section, a "directly competing work" shall be defined as any book-length work on the subject of [be as specific as possible] and intended primarily for distribution and sale to [be as specific as possible] through [specify] channels. The Publisher acknowledges that the Author has in process the following works, provisionally entitled: *[specify]* and agrees that these works do not constitute directly competing works. The Publisher further agrees that the Author's activities as a [specify], and any work that she/he might write or present in connection with the performance of those activities (and not constituting a book-length work for adoption as a primary text in the following courses [specify course titles and curricular level]) shall not be deemed a breach of the provisions of this Section. Nor shall the use of her/his name or likeness in connection with such activities be deemed a breach thereof.

Negotiating Strategy:

The narrower the non-compete, the better. The more precisely you can define what it is you will not do and what it is you are free to do, the less opportunity there will be for misunderstandings. If the publisher expresses a reluctance to more precisely define the boundaries, ask for a quid pro quo — i.e., a parallel commitment from the publisher to refrain from publishing the works of other authors on the same subject. It is highly unlikely that the publisher would entertain such a prospect, but the mere thought may make them more reasonable about the scope of your non-compete.

8. Obligations of the Publisher

Although most publishing contracts are meticulous about detailing the obligations of the author (time being expressly noted as of the essence with respect to the performance of same), they go an equal distance in the opposite direction when it comes to the publisher's obligations. See (8a.) for language regarding publishing obligations in a typical textbook publishing contract.

You'll notice that the publisher has said it will publish the work, but it hasn't said exactly when it will do that, or in what format, or at what price. Nor has it said what, if anything, it will do to market and promote the work.

If the author delivers a completed and acceptable manuscript, he or she will have fulfilled his or her obligations. But his or her compensation comes primarily from commercialization of the work by the publisher; if the publisher doesn't bring the book to market in the agreed upon form and in timely fashion, it should be prepared to forfeit its rights in the work. Watch out for language that would permit the publisher to discharge its obligation to publish simply by making a digital version or print-on-demand edition of the work available.

> ... if the publisher doesn't bring the book to market in the agreed upon form and in timely fashion, it should be prepared to forfeit its rights in the work.

8a. Obligations of the Publisher - typical

PUBLISHING DETAILS. The Publisher agrees, when it has accepted the completed Work and in its judgment the Work and those ancillary materials it considers necessary or desirable are ready for publication, to publish the Work at its expense and to distribute it through the channels and at the prices it considers best suited to the sale of the Work in the specified market. The Publisher shall select formats and title for the Work, and the methods and the timing of the marketing effort. The Author agrees that the Publisher may at its discretion use his or her name, likeness, and biographical data in and in connection with the Work and all future editions or derivative works thereof.

8b. Obligations of the Publisher - better

PUBLISHING DETAILS. The Publisher shall publish the Work at its expense and shall diligently promote, market, and distribute it through such channels and at such prices as are suited to the sale of the Work, all in good faith consultation with the Author. The Publisher shall select the formats and title for the Work, in consultation with the Author. The Publisher shall identify the Author as the author on copies of, and in promotional copy for, the Work and may at its discretion use her name, likeness, and biographical data in and in connection with the Work and all future editions or derivative works thereof.

Should the Publisher fail to publish the Work in a printed and bound edition available for distribution in the United States in commercially reasonably quantities within 12 months of the Author's delivery of a complete and acceptable manuscript, the Author may at her election terminate this Agreement by written notice to the Publisher, in which event all rights in the Work shall revert to her and she shall be entitled to retain any amounts previously advanced or paid to her as her sole remedy.

9. Manuscript Submission

It is one thing to be signed to a publishing contract, but unfortunately (and perhaps unfairly) quite another to actually to be published. Most form publishing agreements include a provision like the one in (9a.), reserving to the publisher the discretion to determine at some later date whether or not a tendered manuscript is satisfactory.

Editors come and go and markets change. An open-ended manuscript acceptability standard (like the one in 9a.) can leave you holding an unpublished manuscript. Most form contracts will require that you deliver a completed manuscript that is acceptable to the publisher in form and content. This arguably allows the publisher to reject your completed work for any reason or even for no reason at all (provided only that the publisher is not acting in bad faith).

9a. Manuscript Submission - typical

SUBMISSION OF MANUSCRIPT. The Author will deliver to the Publisher, on or before [date], a complete and legible typewritten manuscript (and word processed text-file) of the Work satisfactory to the Publisher in form and content. If the manuscript for the complete Work is not delivered on or before the date specified above, or if the manuscript is not satisfactory to the Publisher in form or content in the Publisher's sole and absolute discretion, the Publisher may, at its option: (a) allow the Author to finish, correct or improve the manuscript by a date specified by the Publisher, (b) have the manuscript properly prepared by such other Author(s) as it may select and the Publisher may deduct the cost of obtaining such Author's services, whether compensated by fee or royalties, from the Author's royalties or (c) terminate this agreement by written notice to the Author, in which case any manuscript shall be returned and all rights therein shall revert to the Author, and any amounts which may have been advanced to the Author will be promptly refunded to the Publisher. In the event circumstances since the date of this Agreement have, in the sole judgment of the Publisher, caused the market for the Work to change or evaporate, the Publisher may reject the Work. In such event, the Publisher shall so notify the Author. The Author shall be entitled to retain one half the advance specified in Paragraph ___ as a kill fee, all rights in the Work shall revert to the Author, and neither the Author nor the Publisher shall have any further obligations hereunder.

Instead, you should:

- **Strive for an acceptability clause** that requires only that the finished manuscript conform in coverage and quality to the sample chapters provided with your prospectus or, alternatively, a clause that requires the manuscript to be professionally competent and fit for publication.

- **Ask for language** that obliges the publisher to provide you with detailed editorial comments and at least one opportunity to revise.

- **Not permit the publisher** to complete or otherwise use your work and charge any third party costs against your account without your consent.

"Do you think my book on ants will start a bidding war?"

9b. Manuscript Submission - better

SUBMISSION OF MANUSCRIPT. The Author will deliver the completed Work on or before [date]. The Publisher acknowledges and agrees that the manuscript will be deemed acceptable so long as it professionally competent and fit for publication in the good faith exercise of the Publisher's reasonable judgment.

9c. Manuscript Submission - better still

SUBMISSION OF MANUSCRIPT. The Author will deliver the completed Work on or before [date]. The Publisher acknowledges and agrees that the manuscript will be deemed acceptable so long as it conforms in content, coverage, style, and rigor to the outline and prospectus previously provided (a copy of which is attached hereto as Exhibit 1). In the event the publisher deems any submission not acceptable, it will so advise the Author in writing within 30 days of the date of submission and will describe with particularity the deficiencies therein and the changes required to make the submission acceptable, in which event that Author shall have 30 days to make the required improvements. The Publisher's failure to so advise the Author in the time and manner specified shall be deemed the Publisher's acceptance as to the tendered submission.

Negotiating Strategy:

Don't assume that just because you were offered a contract based upon your tender of a proposal, or even a completed first draft manuscript, that the publisher will necessarily publish the work. If the acquiring editor moves on, you will be back to square one with a new editor who may not have the same level of interest in or commitment to your work. When seeing the work in print is an important objective, make sure you close and lock the publisher's back door.

10. Ancillaries

Watch out also for open-ended commitments to prepare and deliver all manner of non-saleable support materials, like those in (10.).

Negotiating Strategy:

Carefully review the list of ancillaries you are being asked to provide and strike those that you think are not warranted and those that you are not prepared to develop. If nothing else, be sure that the list does not include an open ended catch-all (e.g., any others the publisher considers desirable). And require that, before the publisher is permitted to charge your account for having someone else do what you agreed to do, the publisher must tell you how much that will cost and give you an opportunity to reconsider. Be sure also that the publisher can only recover its actual out-of-pocket costs for outsourcing the work; don't let them recover some of their staff salaries by charging them back to your royalty account. Even for those supplements that are saleable, like study guides or work books, publishers assume that if you don't prepare them you don't get a royalty on sales. But the fact is that these supplements are derivative of your work on the main text, without which there would be no market for or outline for the supplement. For that reason, it is appropriate for you to ask for some portion of the royalties on any saleable supplement that accompanies your work, regardless of whether or not you participated in preparing that supplement.

ANCILLARIES. When requested by the Publisher, and in consideration of royalties to be paid as provided herein, the Author agrees to prepare such non-saleable ancillary materials as instructor's manuals, instructor's editions, keys, test banks, solutions manuals, audio-visual materials, web site content and all such other teaching and learning aids that the Publisher considers necessary or desirable in order to promote the sale of the Work. No separate payment will be made for such aids. If for any reason the Author does not or cannot prepare these teaching aids to meet the Publisher's schedule, the Author agrees that the Publisher may select a person or persons it deems competent to prepare such materials and that the cost shall be charged to the Author's royalty account. In addition, the Publisher may prepare any saleable ancillary materials it deems desirable without the Author's participation, at its own expense, and without separate compensation to the Author.

Keep in mind... the fact is that these supplements are derivative of your work on the main text, without which there would be no market for or outline for the supplement.

11. Editorial Control

The publisher's form agreement will likely reserve exclusively to it a wide range of discretion when it comes to how your work will be edited, published, and marketed.

11a. Editorial Control - typical

EDITING AND DETERMINATIONS. Without attempting to define or limit any other rights it may have under this Agreement, the Publisher expressly reserves the right to, in its sole discretion, to: (i) publish or not publish the Work; (ii) commission, license and/or include or not include any third party materials and/or commissioned materials in the Work; (iii) edit the Work or any revision of it provided that the meaning of the Work is not materially altered; (iv) assess the manufacturing costs for the Work and the size of its market, and decide the number of copies that can be printed economically; (v) publish the Work in one or more volumes, and in any such style or format as the Publisher deems best suited to the sale of the Work; (vi) fix or alter the title, appearance (or omission) and order of the Authors' names, and prices at which the Work shall be sold; (vii) determine the method and means of marketing the Work, the number and destination of free copies, and all other publishing details, including the use of plates, type, film, or other process, the date of publication, the form and format, the style of composition, the size and type of paper to be used, and like details; (viii) keep the Work in print only as long as it deems expedient; and (ix) decide if and when reprints and/or revisions shall be made, how long plates, film, or electronic files shall be preserved, and when they shall be destroyed.

11b. Editorial Control - better

EDITING AND DETERMINATIONS. The Publisher may edit the manuscript in accordance with the Publisher's standard style of capitalization, punctuation, spelling, and usage.

11c. Editorial Control - better still

EDITING AND DETERMINATIONS. The Publisher shall not make any substantive change, addition to, or deletion from the Work without the Author's prior written permission, except for copyediting changes necessary to conform the Work to the Publisher's house style.

Negotiating Strategy:

Textbooks are often disregarded when it comes to promotion and tenure considerations. But if you happen to be at an institution that is willing to take them into account, you want to be certain that a text published with your name on it reflects your professional and scholarly judgment about what ought to be said and how. But you will have to read this part of your contract carefully and will have to push back to maintain any sort of control because publishers write their contracts to preserve for themselves maximum flexibility on these points.

> You will have to read this part of your contract carefully and will have to push back to maintain any sort of control on these points.

12. Warranties and Indemnities of Author

Publishers usually require their authors to make certain representations and warranties about the work submitted — that it isn't libelous, that it doesn't infringe third party copyrights, and so on — using language much like that in (12a.).

This is generally a reasonable request because, in many respects, only the author is in a position to know whether or not the author's work is original and non-infringing. Be careful, however, that these representations apply only to work as supplied by you and not to the work of other contributors or editors. Also, we all know that every editor likes to put his/her mark on a work by changing the title. Be sure that you do not warrant that the title does not infringe trademark or other rights (unless, of course, it is indeed your title and you have taken appropriate steps to clear its use).

Most contracts will also require you to indemnify the publisher for any damage or cost incurred as a result of your breach of the foregoing warranties. It is reasonable for you to ask that such indemnification be limited to defects as determined by a court of competent jurisdiction and also to ask that your obligation to indemnify the publisher be capped at the total royalties and other payments you actually receive from the publisher's exploitation of your work, or that you be added as a named insured on the publisher's media perils policy. While the latter may sound like a happy compromise, understand that the deductibles (for which you would still be liable) are generally very large.

12a. Warranties & Indemnities of Author - typical

AUTHOR WARRANTIES, REPRESENTATIONS, AND INDEMNITIES. The Author hereby warrants and represents that: (i) the Author has the right to enter into this Agreement and to grant the rights herein granted and the Author has not and will not assign, pledge, or encumber such rights; (ii) the Author is the sole Author of the Work and, except for material of others permission for use of which has been obtained by the Author pursuant to Paragraph __, the Work is original and previously unpublished; (iii) the Work is not in the public domain; (iv) neither the Work nor its title will contain any material that would violate or infringe any personal, proprietary, or other right of any person or entity or that would violate any contract of the Author, express or implied, or that would disclose any information given to the Author in confidence or on the understanding it would not be disclosed or published; (v) no material in the Work is inaccurate; (vi) the use of any instruction, material, or formula contained in the Work will not result in injury; and (vii) appropriate warnings will be contained in the Work concerning any particular hazards that may be involved in carrying out experiments described in the Work or involved in the use of instructions, materials, or formulas in the Work, and descriptions of relevant safety precautions. The Author hereby indemnifies and agrees to hold the Publisher, its licensees, and any seller of the Work harmless from any liability, damage, cost, and expense, including reasonable attorney's fees and costs of settlement, for or in connection with any claim, action, or proceeding inconsistent with the Author's warranties or representations herein, or based upon or arising out of any contribution of the Author to the Work. The Publisher will notify the Author of any claim, action, or proceeding, and the Publisher may use counsel of its own selection to defend the same. The Author may participate in the defense, at the Author's own expense, with counsel of the Author's own choosing. The Publisher will have the right to withhold payment of sums otherwise payable to the Author under this or any other agreement with the Author, and to apply the sums withheld to such liability. The warranties, representations, and indemnity of the Author herein will survive termination of this Agreement for any reason and will extend to any licensees, distributors, and assigns of the Publisher.

AUTHOR WARRANTIES, REPRESENTATIONS, AND INDEMNITIES. The Author hereby warrants and represents, with respect only to the Author's contributions to the Work, that: (i) the Author has the right to enter into this Agreement and to grant the rights herein granted and the Author has not and will not assign, pledge, or encumber such rights; (ii) the Author is the sole Author of the Work and, except for material of others permission for use of which has been obtained by the Author pursuant to Paragraph __, the Work is original and previously unpublished; (iii) the Work is not in the public domain; (iv) the Work contains no material that would violate or infringe any personal, proprietary, or other right of any person or entity or that would violate any contract of the Author, express or implied, or that would disclose any information given to the Author in confidence or on the understanding it would not be disclosed or published; (v) to the best of the Author's knowledge no material in the Work is inaccurate; and (vi) the use of any instruction, material, or formula contained in the Work will not result in injury; and appropriate warnings will be contained in the Work concerning any particular hazards that may be involved in carrying out experiments described in the Work or involved in the use of instructions, materials, or formulas in the Work, and descriptions of relevant safety precautions. The Author hereby indemnifies and agrees to hold the Publisher, its licensees, and any seller of the Work harmless from any liability, damage, cost, and expense, including reasonable attorney's fees and costs of settlement, for or in connection with any claim, action, or proceeding based upon a breach (as determined by the final and non-appealable verdict of a court of competent jurisdiction) of the Author's warranties or representations herein. The Publisher will notify the Author of any claim, action, or proceeding, and the Publisher may use counsel of its own selection to defend the same. The Author may participate in the defense, at the Author's own expense, with counsel of the Author's own choosing. The Author shall not be responsible for any settlement of a claim, action, or proceeding with respect to which the Author has reasonably withheld the Author's approval. The Publisher will have the right to withhold its reasonable estimate of the total liability of the Author (including reasonable attorney's fees) from sums otherwise payable to the Author under this or any other agreement with the Author, and to apply the sums withheld to such liability.

Negotiating Strategy:

The publisher may have a limited ability to alter the language in these clauses as a result of the requirements of its policy of insurance. In any event, your exposure under these clauses is largely within your control. If there is something about the nature of your work that makes it susceptible to attack (e.g., it constitutes a largely negative treatment of a business case reflecting poorly on the skills of certain executives), it is in your best interest to be sure that the publisher is fully aware of the issues and that you work closely with the publisher and its media perils insurer to minimize the likelihood of a successful challenge.

AUTHOR WARRANTIES, REPRESENTATIONS, AND INDEMNITIES. The Author hereby warrants and represents, with respect only to the Work as submitted by the Author, that, to the best of the Author's actual knowledge: (i) the Author has the right to enter into this Agreement and to grant the rights herein granted and the Author has not and will not assign, pledge, or encumber such rights; (ii) the Author is the sole Author of the Work and, except for material of others permission for use of which has been obtained by the Author pursuant to Paragraph __, the Work is original and previously unpublished; (iii) the Work is not in the public domain; (iv) and the Work contains no material that would violate or infringe any personal, proprietary, or other right of any person or entity or that would violate any contract of the Author, express or implied, or that would disclose any information given to the Author in confidence or on the understanding it would not be disclosed or published. The Author hereby indemnifies and agrees to hold the Publisher, its licensees, and any seller of the Work harmless from any liability, damage, cost, and expense, including reasonable attorney's fees and costs of settlement, for or in connection with any claim based upon a breach of the Author's warranties or representations herein as determined by the final and non-appealable judgment of a court of competent jurisdiction; provided that the Publisher promptly notifies the Author of any such claim and cooperates with the Author in its defense. The Author shall not be responsible for any settlement of a claim, action, or proceeding with respect to which the Author has reasonably withheld the Author's approval. The Publisher shall add the Author as a named insured on the Publisher's media perils policy of insurance.

If there is something about the nature of your work that makes it susceptible to attack, make sure that the publisher is fully aware .

13. Permissions to Use Other Materials

It is likely that the publisher's form contract will contain language that pushes complete responsibility for clearing permissions onto the author, but at the same time leaves final authority for what constitutes a sufficient license with the publisher. Language like that in (13.) would not be unusual.

But this allocation of responsibility/authority is not especially fair or efficient. The author probably knows much less about clearing rights than does the publisher and probably has not previously dealt with any of the sources from whom permission might be necessary. Conversely, the publisher doubtless has some staffers who deal with permissions regularly and who have already established relationships with many commonly used sources, like stock photo houses and trade magazine publishers. Most established textbook publishers recognize this fact of life and will, if pressed, agree to handle the job of clearing permissions. They may also agree to cover some, or occasionally all, of the cost... or at least to advance the rights payments and recover them out of royalties. More difficult, but still worth trying, is to get them to agree to take and pay for less than rights in all languages and all media throughout the world, the latter being more convenient for them but rarely necessary for most textbooks. In instances where the author will ultimately be called upon to cover the final cost of permissions, up front or out of royalties, it is important for the author to retain a final veto power once the cost of any piece is established against the possibility that it isn't worth what it will cost.

13. Permissions to Use Other Materials - typical

THIRD PARTY PERMISSIONS. The Author shall clearly identify to the Publisher all materials for the Work and related materials that were not created by the Author, or are otherwise subject to legal rights of others. The Author shall be solely responsible for obtaining, at the Author's expense, permissions, releases, and other necessary authorizations, in form satisfactory to the Publisher, for the use of such materials in the Work and related materials in all media and all languages throughout the world.

14. Author's and Publisher's Changes in Proofs

Press time is expensive and must generally be reserved well in advance. So once a publisher commits to launch a book during a particular window of time, it understandably does not want to encounter unexpected delays. For this, and other reasons you can well guess, most publishers include language in their contracts to limit an indecisive author's late-stage discretionary changes. That language would look something like that in (14.).

Understand that this is typically not so much about the cost of alterations as it is about creating a disincentive to the delay they may cause. If you are not one of those folks who cannot ever say this is good enough, you have little to be concerned about.

In our experience and the experience of TAA members, this provision is rarely invoked. Do, however, be sure that "publisher's corrections and errors" are included in the parenthetical carve out along with those of the printer.

14. Proofs - typical

PROOFS. The Author will read and correct proofs of the Work if requested to do so, and return them on the Publisher's schedule. The Publisher will absorb the costs of Author's alterations accepted by the Publisher, unless such costs (excluding costs of printer's errors) exceed ten percent (10%) of the cost of the composition of the Work, in which case the Author will assume the excess cost by deduction from his or her royalty account.

15. Marketing and Promotion

As you can see from the treatment of "publishing details" in **section 8,** the publisher's form agreement will generally reserve exclusively to the publisher sole and absolute discretion for how and when to market and promote your work. And their interests here are understandable – they have a business to run and they need the flexibility to allocate and re-allocate their resources to the purposes that make the most economic sense at any given time. This is generally not perfectly predictable – authors are sometimes late with manuscripts; reviewers are sometimes late with comments; other unforeseeable gremlins creep in from time to time. But just as it is reasonable for the publisher to maintain a fair degree of control over how it manages its internal resources, it is equally unreasonable to refuse to make any commitment at all. That said, for whatever reasons publishers will rarely make firm commitments in this area or changes to their contract language.

An experienced author with a lot of bargaining leverage can sometimes make inroads here. More often, however, the publisher will only commit to consult with an author on marketing and promotion decisions *(see "Better" example in section 8)*. And if a publisher seems to be holding fast to its contract language as initially proposed, sometimes they will agree to put their marketing intentions in a side letter. This may or may not be enforceable as a matter of law, depending on the timing of the letter in relation to the contract effective date and exactly what is written in each. But sometimes just having it on paper is enough to remind a conscientious and ethical publisher of promises made in some cases several years before they were to be delivered on.

More often... the publisher will only commit to consult with an author on marketing and promotion decisions.

16. Royalty Reporting and Payment

It is most typical in textbook publishing for the publishers to account for and pay royalties twice yearly. Those on a calendar year do this for the periods January-June and July-December. Those who have elected a different fiscal year will adjust accordingly. Often they will take up to four months from the close of a period to provide the accounting and corresponding payment. In this day and age, there is little justification for such a long delay. That said, many publishers are accounting to thousands of authors for tens of thousands of products and their systems are necessarily highly automated. So it is one thing to get them to agree to account to you on a schedule that departs from their norm, and an entirely different thing to get them to actually do it. This is the language from a typical textbook publishing contract with regard to royalty reporting and payment:

"Apparently, all the people whom we thought would purchase this book have up and left the country."

16. Reports & Payments - typical

REPORTS AND PAYMENT. The Publisher shall send the Author semi-annual statements of account in the months of April and October covering the six-month periods ending the preceding December 31 and June 30, respectively, and shall pay with each statement the amount due under this Agreement, less any charges. The Publisher may recover any advances or other charges to the Author's account, under this Agreement or otherwise, by withholding payments otherwise due the Author under any agreement between the Author and the Publisher.

So, as unlikely as you are to get meaningful changes in the publisher's reporting and payment language, the one change you should absolutely work to get concerns the language here in (16.). This concerns a concept called "cross-collateralization," which is the publisher's right and ability to recover charges against one book or edition from royalties otherwise due on another. Each book you agree to write, and each revision you agree to prepare, should stand on its own economic legs. There is no good reason a publisher should be able to offset its risk at your expense by covering its downside on one project with your upside on another, even if they are related to one another but especially if one project is unrelated to the other. As just one fairly absurd consequence of the cross-collateralization provision, you could on December 15 get an advance of $25,000 against a contract you just signed for a new book only to have that $25,000 deducted from the royalties you would otherwise have received three months later in March from the sales of your successful already published book.

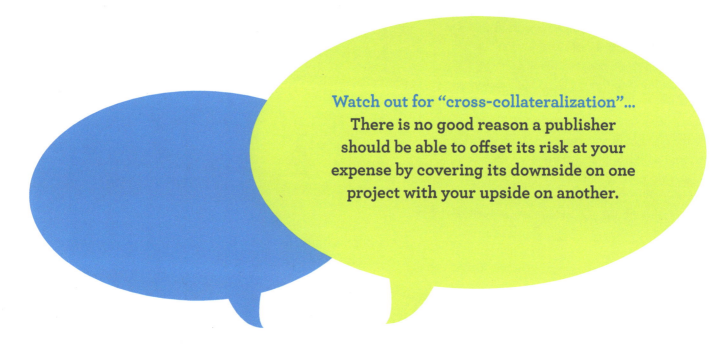

Watch out for "cross-collateralization"...
There is no good reason a publisher should be able to offset its risk at your expense by covering its downside on one project with your upside on another.

17. Inspection of Publisher's Accounts by Author

Most publishers will agree to cooperate in a voluntary audit of an author's royalty account, whether or not the publishing contract obliges them to do so. The alternative – to refuse to cooperate and wait to be sued for underpayment of royalties – is, though uncommon, a very undesirable outcome for the publisher, which would likely result in what would amount to a court compelled and supervised audit on a much faster and less flexible schedule than would otherwise be probable. That said, it will be more efficient to do an audit if the contract anticipates the possibility and details the protocol. If, however, you ask for an audit clause and allow the publisher to provide it, it will most likely look something like that in (17.).

The first thing the publisher will do is to attempt to limit the look back period to something between one and three years (two years shown in example 17). The applicable statute of limitations in most jurisdictions is more like six years, so if you agree to this limitation you will be giving up half or more of your potential recovery at any point in time. The publisher may also attempt to bar you from arranging for your audit on a contingent fee basis. This may, as a practical matter, keep you from being able to afford an audit as the time and expense is otherwise substantial. And finally, the publisher will want you to bear the expense of any audit. But a more reasonable compromise would have the publisher reimburse you if the error is found to be in their favor in an amount of more than 5% of the amount shown to be due. And, of course, the publisher should make any payment shown to be due promptly together with interest on the underpaid amount at a reasonable rate.

17. Audit - typical

AUDIT. For a period of two (2) years following the issue of each statement, if the Author has a good faith basis to believe that there has been an under-reporting of royalties properly due and owing, the Publisher shall make such books and records available for inspection by a certified public accountant representing the Author (provided such accountant agrees to be bound by the confidentiality provision contained in this Agreement and provided further that no such audit may be conducted on a contingency fee basis) for the purpose of verifying the correctness of the payments made with respect to those items for which the Author believes there has been an under-reporting. Following such two (2) year period each such statement shall be deemed uncontestable, binding and not subject to audit by the Author. Such inspections may be made upon ninety (90) days' prior written notice at reasonable times and at the place where the Publisher's relevant records are kept, and shall not be conducted more than once each calendar year. Each such statement rendered hereunder may only be the subject of one audit. The Author shall bear all expenses associated with such audit.

18. Author's Copies

The publisher will offer you some complimentary copies of your work upon its publication – typically from 6 to 10 copies – using language like that in (18.).

But once a textbook has been developed and published, the cost of manufacturing a few extra copies is negligible, so don't be bashful about asking for more copies, especially if you intend to use them to help promote the book. If you hope to be able to sell copies of your book directly to attendees at speeches or professional presentations or workshops, ask your publisher for the right to re-sell copies together with the ability to purchase more for that purpose at the publisher's best available discount to resellers.

19. Revisions of the Book

Textbook publishing contracts anticipate and provide for regular revision of the work. Generally, the timing is up to the publisher and when request for a revision is made the new edition will be governed by the same terms that covered the previous edition. This protects each party from being held hostage to the whims of the other. The Revisions example in (19.) illustrates the language regarding revisions from a typical textbook publishing contract.

You'll see that most contracts also anticipate that there will come a time when the author is no longer able or willing to continue. When this happens, the publisher is given the right to proceed with the assistance of another author of its selection. In recognition of the fact that the incoming writer gets a head start from the work done by her predecessor, the contract author gets a continuing right to royalties for some period of time. Sometimes the contract sets out a step down period (like the half rate for one edition specified in 19.); sometimes the contract says only that the cost of hiring a substitute will be deducted from the sums otherwise due the author. You have some negotiating room here to improve upon the duration and amounts of any step-down arrangement and you will rarely have better leverage to do that than right at the outset of your relationship.

18. Author's Copies - typical

AUTHOR'S COPIES. Upon publication, the Publisher will give the Author, without charge, ten (10) copies of the Work. If more than one person signs this Agreement as the Author, each will be given five (5) copies without charge. The Author may purchase additional copies of the Work at a discount of twenty-five percent (25%) from the Publisher's catalog price, directly from the Publisher, for personal use but not for resale.

REVISIONS. The Author will revise the Work when called upon by the Publisher to do so. Except as expressly set forth herein, all the terms of this Agreement will apply to each revision as though it were the Work being published for the first time. If the Author refuses, fails, or is unable to deliver a revision to the Publisher within a reasonable time of the Publisher's written request, the Publisher may have the revision prepared or completed by others, give them authorship credit, and the Publisher will pay the Author, or the Author's legal successors, one-half of the applicable royalty and payments specified herein with respect to the first revision in which the Author does not participate, and nothing with respect to any subsequent edition. If the Author does not participate in any revision, the Author will not have the right to participate in any later revision, except under a specific written agreement with the Publisher.

20. Assignments and Successors

As a general rule of contract law, most contracts are assignable unless they say they are not. Since the publisher intends to contract with you personally, in reliance upon your stature and reputation and demonstrated ability to write, to prepare and deliver the manuscript for the work, the contract will say as much in language like that in (20.).

Although you may hear it argued that publishers should likewise not be able to sell or assign the contract either, as a practical matter it would be a very extraordinary circumstance where they would agree to such a restriction on their ability to sell all or a part of their business and, as much as the sale of your contract to another publisher may disadvantage you if the other publisher has a competing list, you will probably have to find another way to manage this risk.

ASSIGNMENT. This Agreement shall be binding upon and for the benefit of the Author and the Author's heirs, executors, administrators, and assigns, and to the Publisher and its successors and assigns. The Publisher may assign this Agreement in whole or in part. The Author may assign his or her royalty rights in this Agreement with written permission of the Publisher, which shall not be unreasonably withheld.

21. Reversion

Most publishing contracts include a provision anticipating the possibility that the book, if published, may eventually be allowed to go out-of-print. Because you stand to profit from your work for only so long as the publisher continues to promote and market it and to keep it available in reasonable quantities sufficient to supply the market demand, you will want the contract to ensure that if the work is allowed to go out of stock and out of print, that the rights will be reverted to you so that you can take it elsewhere. In times past, when books were sold only in hard copy form, it was relatively easy to set the trigger for a reversion. With the migration to digital copies, the publishers have adjusted their language in a way that is probably overreaching, as you can see in the typical textbook contract language in (21.).

This language would probably be interpreted to permit the publisher to hold the rights to your book so long as it had one digital copy available to supply print-on-demand orders. This is probably unreasonable. For its part, the publisher will not want to risk a forfeiture of its investment and rights if the book is temporarily stocked out (especially if this results from an unexpected high demand) and so will want some sort of notice and reasonable opportunity to cure. Both of these concerns can be reasonably addressed if youand your publisher can agree that if royalties drop below a certain specified amount for some number of consecutive royalty periods, the contract will be terminable at your election by notice to the publisher, whereupon the rights will automatically revert to you.

You may be inclined to resist spending much of your leverage to negotiate the terms of a divorce during the courtship, but if things do not go as planned and this provision becomes important, it will almost certainly be close to last on the publisher's priority list — that publisher will have little or no interest in your plight and little or no incentive to be responsive to an earnest plea to "please release me..." Your only real opportunity to solve this potential problem is to insist at the outset that the agreement precisely define when the work must be reverted (and not leave this to the discretion of the publisher) and make the reversion process as automatic as it can possibly be.

21. Reversion - typical

OUT-OF-PRINT. If, at any time after two years from the original publication date, the Work is out of print for a period of six or more months, the Publisher will, after written request from the Author, either restore the Work to print within six months or, upon payment to the Publisher of any sums owed by the Author, return to the Author all rights granted herein; except, however, that any licenses previously granted will continue in effect and the Publisher will continue to receive its share of the proceeds from any such licenses. The Work will be deemed in print so long as it is in stock or on sale in any edition, print or digital, or revised edition of the Publisher or its licensees or under contract for publication in any edition or revised edition. Notwithstanding the foregoing, the Publisher will retain all rights to the original graphic material included in the Work.

22. Choice of Law/Venue

Like most contracts of any sort, the typical textbook publishing contract will specify which state law will be applied to its interpretation and enforcement and will probably also specify where any disputes are to be resolved, as shown in (22.).

As often as not, New York is selected for both choice of law and choice of venue. That state has a well developed body of statutory and case law concerning publishing contracts and there is really no good reason to object to its selection for the applicable law. As to venue, however, it is likely to be much less convenient and more expensive for authors than would be other possible venues, but unless you have a good bit of leverage, you are not likely to get any movement on this point.

22. Choice of Law/Venue - typical

CHOICE OF LAW/VENUE. This Agreement shall be governed by and construed in accordance with the laws of the State of New York without reference to conflict of law principles there under which would require the application of the laws of another jurisdiction. Any dispute arising under this Agreement shall be resolved in the state or federal courts of New York County, New York, and each party hereto waives any objection to venue and hereby submits to the personal jurisdiction of such courts.

23. Signature Block

The contract will close with a signature block where each party signifies its/his/her assent to the terms of the contract.

The only significant thing to watch here is to be sure that the identification of the party signing for the author matches what is set out in the recitals; i.e., if the author is entering the contract in her personal capacity, that she signs as an individual and provides her personal tax ID number; and that if she is entering the contract through a personal services company, that she signs not in her personal capacity but in her capacity as an authorized representative of the company and provides not her personal tax ID but the employer identification number for her company.

23. Signature Block - typical

In witness whereof, the Author and Publisher have signed this contract on the dates following their signatures.

Author: _____

Date:_____

Publisher:_____

Signature

Name/Title:_____

Date:_____

Conclusion

Odds are, you will not prevail on all of these issues. But odds are equally as good that you will not lose on all of them either. In any event, you will not get that for which you do not ask. So ask away... at the end of the day you will have a better deal and a more informed relationship with your publisher.

20 Questions
to Ask Your Editor

What follows is a list of 20 questions (more or less) that you can employ to learn more about your publisher's plans for, and expectations of, your work — information that will help you evaluate your leverage and your editor's weaknesses. Ask them in the context of negotiating a book contract and the editor will evade them, hedge, or refuse to answer. Ask them after the editor has indicated an interest in your work but before you engage in active contract-focused negotiations — in the context of learning more about your editor and publisher, more about their list and their business, more about the market and your potential competition — and you may catch the editor still in his or her selling mode. Ask them yourself and in person or over the phone.

Negotiations may be formal and may be best handled by your attorney or agent in order to preserve your relationship with your editor. But information gathering will be most effective if you do it in person. A question perceived as innocuous when asked by you will be viewed with suspicion if posed by your agent or attorney. It may take some prodding, probing, wheedling, and cajoling, but the information you gather will prove valuable so take copious notes.

1 **How long have you been with the publisher?** Editors move from house to house and it will be helpful to know how long your editor has been in his or her current position.

2 **Where were you before?** The experience an editor gained at other houses will tell you something about his or her knowledge of the market and the business.

Your first task is to loosen up the editor with some questions about his or her background. Get the editor talking freely and you are well on your way.

3 **Did you come up through the sales side or through editorial?** The editor with a sales background will have a significantly different negotiating focus from the editor with an editorial background.

4 **Tell me about your current list. How many titles are there? What disciplines? What curricular level? What are your lead titles? What sort of market share do they have? Are any of them market leaders?** The answers to these questions will tell you something about your editor's place in the pecking order and about how much attention your project is likely to get. Next, find out how important your project is to the editor's bonus. (No editor will knowingly tell you, but the answers to these next questions may provide a few clues).

5 **How many new books do you sign in a typical year?** The answer to this question will tell you something about the editors annual signing goals.

6 **How many new books have you signed so far this year?** The answer to this question will give you some idea of where the editor is in relation to his or her goals. If the editor is close to his/her annual average, it could well be that signing you will make the difference between earning or not earning a bonus. You will probably never know for certain how important your project is, but you may at least get a clue.

7 **How would you envision positioning my book vis-a-vis the competition?** This will tell you what your editor sees as your work's competitive advantages — information that will prove useful should you decide to approach other publishers with your project.

8 **Who are your principal competitors in this market?** If you have not already submitted to these competitors, you should seriously consider doing so immediately. The best leverage you can have in

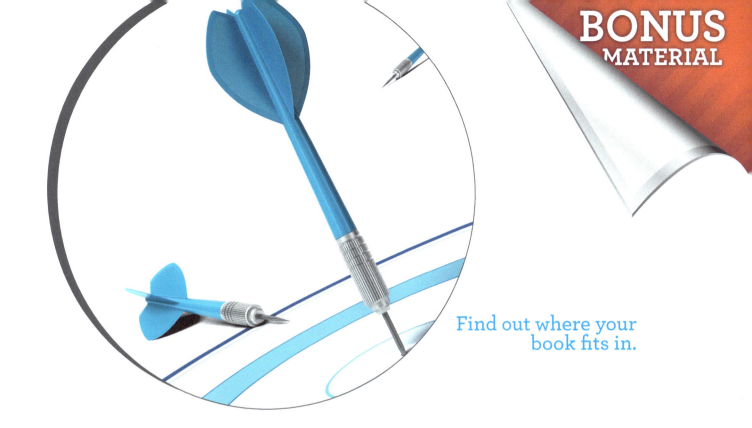

Find out where your book fits in.

negotiating a book contract is to know that there is another interested publisher in the wings.

9 **Do you have any titles (published or signed) similar to mine?** For obvious reasons, you want to know if the editor will have divided loyalties. Moreover, when it comes time to talk about the scope of your non-compete clause, it is very helpful to be able to point out specifically that the publisher is not similarly constrained.

10 **If the proposal or partial manuscript has been reviewed,** check the reviews to see who is identified as a competitor. Again, you want to know about the other publishers who might also be interested in your work.

Get the numbers. The answers to the following questions will help you back into a reasonable advance against royalties.

11 **How big a market are we talking about?** This will give you a sense of how the publisher views your book and whether you both see it the same way.

12 **What sort of market penetration does the publisher generally expect with a new book?** In combination with the answer to Question 11, this will give you a way of corroborating the editor's sales projections.

13 **How many units would an average book do in the market for which my book is targeted? First year? Lifetime? How many do you think the market leader does?** The answers to these questions, once you know the cover price, will let you estimate revenues and royalties so that you can make a credible, objectively supportable request for advances.

14 **How many units does a book like mine have to do to break even?** The answer to this question will tell you at what volume the publisher covers its costs.

15 **How many units would my book have to do before you would consider it a roaring success?** The answer to this question will tell you at what point the publisher has made its customary margin. The break-even volume and the volume necessary to a **target margin** are natural break points for a sliding royalty scale. Consider accepting the rate first offered up to break even, but ask for a higher rate up to the target margin, and ask for the moon beyond that.

How would you see my book priced? As noted, this information helps you project revenues and royalties, but it also will tell you something about the titles your editor views as competitive — because they will necessarily fall in the same price range.

16 **Do you think it would travel well?** If the editor says no, then it will be very hard for him/her to push for exclusive, perpetual foreign and translation rights.

17 **Tell me about your foreign sales ability? Sub-rights licensing (translations and adaptations)? New media capability?** Again, rights that the editor is not positioned to aggressively exploit should not be part of the package.

Get the promotion plan.

18 **What would you envision doing to promote a book like mine? How many pages in the promotional brochure? Full color? How big a mailing? How many review copies and comp copies? Presentation at sales conference? Author appearance? Journal ads? Anything else?** Most publishing contracts say very little indeed about what the publisher will do to market and promote your work. If you get a sales pitch from the editor, make an effort to reduce it to writing and reference it in the publishing contract.

Check the back door.

19 **Roughly what percent of the titles you sign actually make it into print?** The answer to this question will tell you how important it is to introduce an objective acceptability standard into the manuscript delivery clause.

20 **Bonus Question!** **Is there anything else I should know about you or about how you see my book fitting into your list?** If your editor is still talking, you should still be taking notes.

You will not get answers to all of these questions. And you will not get answers to any of them without a fair amount of prodding. But the time and effort you spend will tell you volumes about your editor and will pay many dividends when the time comes to negotiate that contract.

Resources:

View these online resources @TAAonline.net

Textbook Author Survey

A survey of 403 textbook authors by TAA and Digital Book Pioneer and Industry Expert June Jamrich Parsons. TAAonline.net/2015-textbook-author-survey

What to Consider Before Signing Your First Textbook Contract

Advice from veteran textbook authors Mike Kennamer and Steven Barkan from their 2014 TAA Conference Roundtable, *What I Wish I Had Known Before I Signed My First Textbook Contract.* http://blog.taaonline. net/2014/06/what-to-consider-before-signing-your-first-textbook-contract

How to Protect Yourself from Lower Textbook Royalties from Foreign Sales

How to avoid being caught in "inter-company" sales by being diligent when negotiating contracts. http://blog.taaonline. net/2011/01/how-to-protect-yourself-from-lower-textbook-royalties-from-foreign-sales

TAA Textbook Contract Review Grants

These grants, available to members and non-members, cover the cost of hiring an intellectual property attorney to review your first textbook contract. TAAonline.net/grants

Wood Herron & Evans Publishing/Media Practice

View a list of the company's soft-side intellectual property matters that make up its robust publishing and media practice, such as drafting and negotiation of all manner of publishing contracts, copyright matters, rights clearance and permissions, and more. www.whe-law.com/practices/publishingmedia

Glossary of Terms

advance: A pre-payment of royalties to be earned upon the publication of your textbook, recouped out of the royalties first accrued from the commercial exploitation of your work.

all rights assignment: (contrast work-for-hire and assignment of book publishing rights) common to many textbook contracts is a grant of rights that consists of an assignment of all rights (including but not limited to copyrights) in the work to the publisher. This grant is in contrast to, and better, for the author than an acknowledgement that the work is agreed to be a work-made-for-hire. It is less favorable than a grant more limited in scope (e.g., a grant of book publishing rights).

ancillaries and supplementary works: these are works separate from, but intended to support, a primary textbook (e.g., student study guide, instructor's manual, test bank). They may be saleable or not. And they may be derivative or not. If they are not saleable, they will probably be covered by the contract for the basic test and there will be no separate compensation for creating them. If they are saleable, they will probably be the subject of a separate contract that may provide for a fee or royalty.

author alterations (AA): these are changes proposed to proof copies at the discretion of the author. The cost of these changes at this stage of the production process in excess of some predetermined threshold may be charged back against the author.

bundling: this is a marketing strategy adopted by publishers (predominantly at the higher ed level) to sell more product for each adoption. In this strategy, several stand alone products are sold together as a bundle for a bundle price that is less than the sum of the individual prices of the components. The proceeds from that sale are then allocated across the components on some basis. It is best for the author if the basis of allocation is something objectively measurable, like page counts or relative stand alone list prices. If the publisher is allowed absolute discretion to determine the allocation the result may be subject to unfair manipulation.

break even vs. target margin: break even is the number of copies your book must sell to cover the publisher's upfront investment in publishing it. The publisher's target margin is the rate of return it hopes to achieve on average with the books it publishes. The unit volume of sales necessary to accomplish each of these objectives represent natural triggers for escalating royalty rates.

choice of law vs. choice of venue: because contract law varies from state to state, it is common in all contracts for the parties to specify which state's law will be used to interpret the contract. This removes one potential point of contention and some uncertainty but is otherwise of relatively little consequence most of the time. Choice of venue is, in contrast, an agreement about where disputes will be litigated and it can have a material adverse impact on one party or the other.

complimentary copies (comps): these are copies provided at no cost to the author on first publication of the work. Ask for more than are offered – they are cheap to produce.

conditional grant of rights: regardless of the scope of the grant of rights, if it is conditioned upon the publisher's full and timely performance of its obligations under the contract, then a material default by the publisher will constitute a failure of the condition, which will nullify the grant and arguably provide the author with an infringement claim as opposed to just a claim for breach of contract. The publisher will almost certainly not volunteer this and will probably resist your attempt to add it if they understand the implications...but you will never know if you don't ask.

copyedit: means to edit the manuscript for punctuation, spelling, grammatical structure, and conformance to the publisher's house style. It does not encompass making or suggesting changes that alter the meaning or substance of the text. It is common for publishers to reserve the right to copyedit the manuscript but they should not make substantive edits without the consent of the author, especially for works targeted at the higher end of the curriculum.

corporation/limited liability company: alternative forms of independent legal entities that can be created under state law to shield the owner's personal assets from liability for the obligations of the business and to accomplish other objectives. A discussion of the pros and cons of each is beyond the scope of this publication. Suffice to say that you should get competent professional advice before proceeding.

cross-collateralized: Recoverable from royalties earned by other titles that you might have written or might yet write for the same publisher.

custom publishing: this is another marketing strategy designed to sell more product and displace potential used book sales by preparing a special product for a single adoption that has been cut down, supplemented, or changed from an existing standalone product. It is subject to the same allocation problem as a "bundle" and may be treated separately or together with bundling in the contract.

derivative work: this is a term of art in copyright law, meaning a work based upon one or more preexisting works, such as a translation or any other form in which a work may be recast, transformed, or adapted. A work consisting of editorial revisions, annotations, elaborations, or other modifications, which, as a whole, represent an original work of authorship, is a "derivative work." Under US copyright law, only the copyright owner has the right to make or authorize the creation of works that are derivative of a copyrighted work.

electronic rights: this term has come to serve as an amorphous (and somewhat inaccurate) reference for the right to exploit a copyrightable work in any digital medium, including not only electronic, but also magnetic and optical. It can refer to anything from a database, to a PDF, to an eBook, to an integrated learning system. Because it can mean many things, the best practice is to define it in your contract.

grant: A payment intended to cover some or all of the out-of-pocket costs of research and/or manuscript preparations. It is generally not recouped out of accrued royalties and may or may not be refundable in the even the manuscript is rejected.

grant of rights clause: Spells out the breadth of rights being acquired by the publisher – and there is a broad range of possibilities here.

indemnification: in publishing contracts is usually required by the publisher from the author for any breach of the representations or warranties. Watch out, however, for language that holds the author accountable for not only actual breaches but also for breaches that are only alleged.

list (as in an editor's list): the group of books for which an editor is responsible, generally limited to one or not more than a couple fields.

market share: this is the share of the entire market for books in a particular subject at a particular curricular level that any given book enjoys.

net receipts: this is generally understood to be cash actually received by the publisher less some offsets. But there is no universally accepted list of the permitted offsets (like credits, returns, taxes, and shipping expenses), so it is important that the term be precisely defined in your contract.

non-compete provision: States that during the life of the agreement the author will not without the prior written consent of the publisher participate in the preparation or publication of any directly competing work.

option (or next-book-option) clause: a clause that requires the author to submit his/her next book-length proposal to the publisher before offering it to any other publisher. More common to trade contracts than to textbook contracts, it nevertheless sometimes finds its way into a textbook contract. Authors should endeavor to strike this provision because it unreasonably restricts their freedom of contract and undermines their ability to deal with other publishers who might be more appropriate choices to publish their next work.

out-of-stock (OS), out-of-print (OP) (or OS/OP): a work that is out-of-stock (temporarily unavailable) is not necessarily out-of-print (flagged for no reprints); somewhat of an anachronism now, this used to be the status commonly used to trigger reversion. With the evolution of eBooks and on demand printing, however, inventory is no longer a meaningful metric for measuring a publisher's enthusiasm for any book in its list.

permission/rights clearance: the process for ensuring, with respect to the inclusion of any third party content in your book, that you have secured the rights necessary to do so or have established that your use is permissible as a fair use or under some other legally recognized exception to the exclusive rights of the copyright owner. Most publishing contracts will place this obligation initially on the author at the author's sole expense, but this allocation of burden and expense is often negotiable.

personal services company/loan out company: these are terms alternatively used to refer to companies sometimes established by authors through which they intend to conduct their writing businesses. The company can take the legal form of a corporation or a limited liability company. Authors who do this generally do it for tax and estate planning purposes. But there are tricks to doing it correctly and traps for the unwary. Get professional advice before you decide on or execute this strategy.

preamble: The paragraph at the top of the contract where the parties are identified, the date of the agreement is noted, and sometimes the purpose is described.

printer/publisher error (PE): these are changes proposed to proof copies by the author that result from errors made by the compositor or the publisher. They should not be counted in the chargeback calculation. Some contracts limit this category to printer errors and do not, though they should, expressly include publisher errors.

recitals: clauses that are used in some contracts, after the preamble and before the substantive provisions of the contract, usually beginning with "Whereas" and ending with "Now Therefore." These clauses are intended to provide background that will assist in interpretation of the substantive provisions that follow. Technically, they are not a binding part of the contractual obligations because they appear before the language that says "the parties, each in consideration for the promises of the other, hereby agree as follows:..." Best practice is to make sure that any matter of substance is not addressed only in the recitals.

representation: a representation in a contract is a promise about the current state of what is being represented. Contrast this with a warranty, which concerns the future. In practice, however, representations and warranties are treated together in publishing contracts and no effort is made to separate or distinguish them.

returns: unlike most consumer products, books have historically been sold by publishers to retailers on a 100% returnable basis. The thinking was that books have no chance of selling through unless they are actually on the bookseller's shelf and by agreeing to accept all returns the publisher eliminates one factor that might cause the bookseller to under order. The consequence of this practice is that many of the copies initially recorded as sold come back later as returns, and any royalties paid on sales are later recouped on returns.

reversion: if and when the market for a work no longer justifies its continued publication by the publisher, then the publisher should terminate the contract and revert all rights to the author. The question is, what is the trigger for this reversion obligation. (See OS/OP)

rights sale vs. product sale: a rights sale (or subrights transaction) involves the grant of a license to a third party to exercise one of the rights otherwise controlled by the publisher–creating and publishing a translation is a classic example. In this sort of transaction, the publisher has no cost of development, manufacture, or distribution to recover and so typically splits the proceeds equally with the author. Contract a product sale, where the publisher does incur these costs upfront and so typically pays a much lower royalty on the proceeds, generally from 10-15%.

satisfactory manuscript: under the language of most publishing contracts, the author will not have fulfilled his/her obligations until he/she has delivered a manuscript that is satisfactory. The question is, how do we decide when and if a manuscript qualifies? See discussion of this issue in the text.

sole or absolute discretion: this is simultaneously more, and less, than what most authors think it is. On the one hand, it gives publishers the authority to make a decision for any reason or for no reason at all. On the other hand, notwithstanding the incorporation of the word "absolute," it does not permit the publisher to make a decision in bad faith because the common law in most states will impute in every contract an obligation on the part of each party to deal with the other fairly and in good faith.

subsidiary rights: Rights subsidiary to the publisher's principal line of business.

tiered royalty structure: A base rate up to the publisher's break even volume, a higher rate on sales over break even, and a higher rate still on sales over the volume at which the publisher achieves its target margin.

time is of the essence: the general rule of law is that performance within a reasonable time of the time and date specified for performance will constitute satisfactory performance, with what is reasonable being determined by industry practice and convention. If you want the date and time in the contract to be enforced strictly, then you need to specify that "time is of the essence." You will likely see this phrase used in connection with an author's deadlines in the contract, but it will not generally be applied to the publisher unless you press for it.

title/work: these terms are used interchangeably to refer to a particular work of expression, without regard to the medium in which it is reproduced.

travel (as in "your book will travel well"): rights can be granted on a country-by-country basis. If your book is the sort that may sell well in other countries, we say it will "travel well."

warranty: a warranty in a contract is a promise that what is being warranted will or will not happen in the future. Contrast this with a representation, which concerns matters as they presently stand. In practice, however, representations and warranties are treated together in publishing contracts and no effort is made to separate or distinguish them.

work-for-hire: The publisher is deemed the author and sole owner for copyright purposes, and the author irrevocably grants to the publisher all right, title and interest (including, without limitation, all copyrights throughout the world and all other legal and equitable rights in all media, whether now known or hereafter invented) to the work.

Contact Us:

Stephen E. Gillen, Partner   (sgillen@whe-law.com)

Direct: (513) 707-0470 | Fax: (513) 241-6234 | sgillen@whe-law.com

2700 Carew Tower | 441 Vine Street | Cincinnati, OH 45202-2917 | www.whe-law.com

---

Textbook & Academic Authors Association (TAA)

P.O. Box 367, Fountain City, Wisconsin 54629

Phone: (727) 563-0020 | Email: info@TAAonline.net | Website: TAAonline.net

Join the TAA Authoring Community at TAAonline.net/join

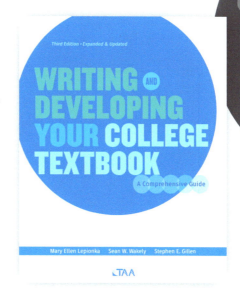